Copyright © 2024 by Camille S. Campbell

All rights reserved.

This publication, or any part thereof, may not be reproduced or distributed in any format, including photocopying, recording, or other electronic or mechanical methods, without the prior written consent of the publisher, except for the use of quotations in book reviews.

Illustrations by Lilia Martyniuk

Colors of Ukraine

The story of Ukrainian artist Maria Prymachenko

Maria ran across the meadow of wildflowers,
over the golden wheat fields
and down the rolling hill.

Honk, honk, honk!

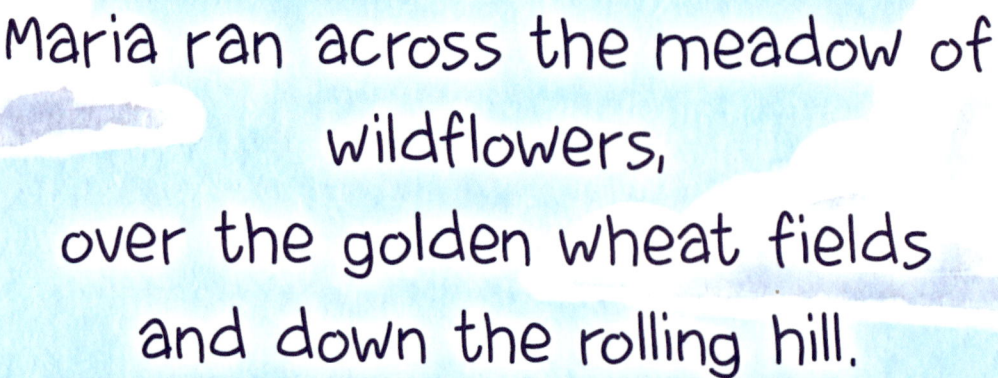

The gaggle of geese trailed after Maria, eager to splash and play at the riverbank.

As Maria waited for the grazing geese, she drew flowers onto the sparkling sand.

Maria started to paint bold blue asters, white moon flowers that bloom at midnight, and yellow sunflowers that smile in the morning.

One day, colors faded from Maria's life.
She fell ill with polio,
and could no longer walk.

To cheer her up, Mama read her a big book filled with Ukrainian folktales.

There were brave girls taming beasts by strumming golden lutes.

Magical eggs cracked to reveal blazing birds with wings of fire.

Mama would tell Maria:

"You are a girl made of many colors—
Sun-yellow Hope,
Ocean-blue Faith,
Poppy-red Determination,
and Golden Love.

Always remember the colors in your heart!"

Darkness turned to color,
Tears of sadness
watered the flowers of joy.

bears that wore crescents like necklaces, and yellow cows with red polka dots.

Maria played with a pesky monkey, riding a four-headed beast.

The beast stole her basket full of strawberries and ate so many that its wings turned red.

During the day,
Maria found joy through painting.
Colors seemed to burst
from the tips of her fingers.
They flowed from her heart
like an endless waterfall.

When the holidays came, white snow sprinkled down from the sky, covering the cottages like powdered sugar.

Maria painted Santa Claus on a flying sled, bringing the pinetree to her village.

Mama taught her how to make gingerbread to welcome a lucky New Year.

It seemed like a New Year's miracle, when Maria took her first fragile steps.

Sun-yellow Hope,
and Ocean-blue Faith,
Poppy-red Determination
and Golden Love,

helped Maria's dream come true.

stitched capes that looked like peacock plumage, and made dresses bright as butterfly wings.

Her designs grew so popular that Maria was invited to an exhibition in the capital of Ukraine, Kyiv.

As she prepared for her first exhibition, Maria felt terribly nervous.

How can my paintings compare to the art in the big city? she wondered.

Moments before the show opened, Maria remembered that when she was sick, art brought colors and joy back into her life.

When Maria unveiled her art, she couldn't believe the reaction. Visitors oohed and ahhed. Guests formed lines to see her paintings.

Word soon spread about her talent. Maria Prymachenko became the most famous artist in all of Ukraine.

www.ingramcontent.com/pod-product-compliance
Lightning Source LLC
Chambersburg PA
CBRC091453160426
43209CB00023B/1882